THE RIDGEWAY

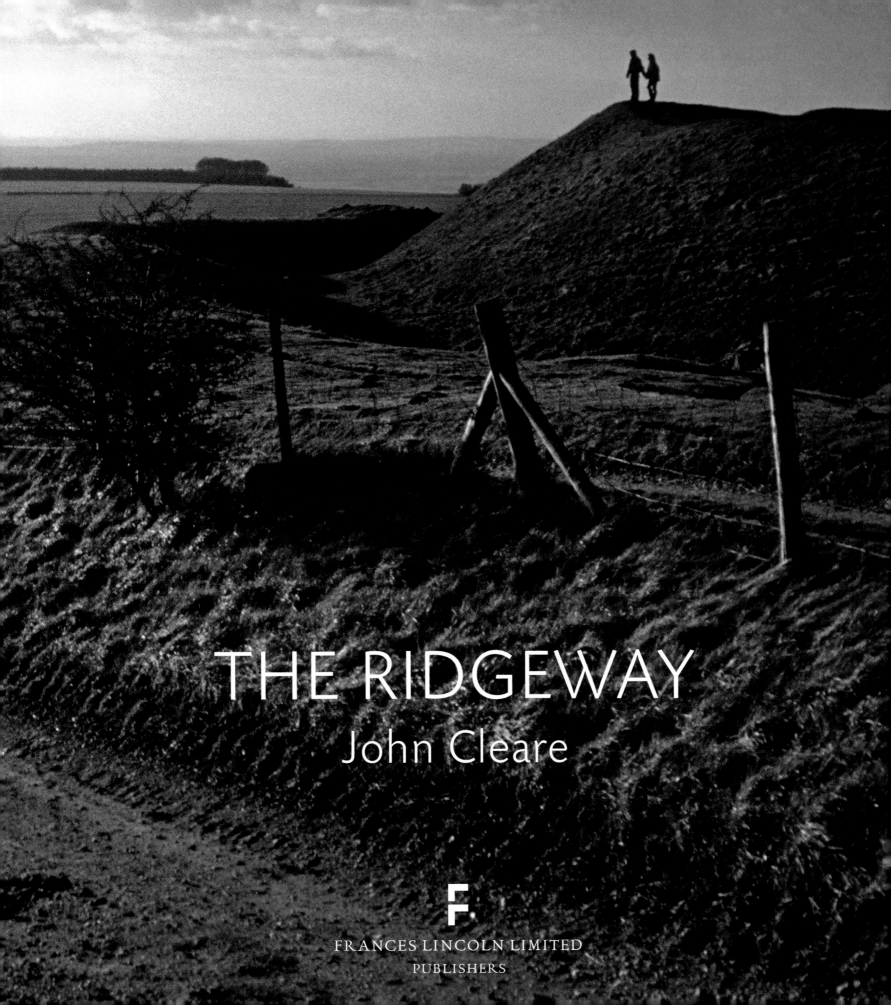

THE RIDGEWAY

John Cleare

F.

FRANCES LINCOLN LIMITED

PUBLISHERS

The Ridgeway
Frances Lincoln Limited
4 Torriano Mews
Torriano Avenue
London NW5 2RZ
www.franceslincoln.com

ISBN: 978-0-7112-3035-4

Printed and bound in China

9 8 7 6 5 4 3 2 1

This book is dedicated to all those who, over the
centuries, have travelled The Ridgeway and to
those who will follow it in years to come.

I am indebted to my good friends Ian Howell, Martin
Andrew and Mike and Sue Esten. Your company, advice,
inspiration and hospitality smoothed my path and added
so much to the pleasure of my task.

Also to another friend, the talented aerial photogra-
pher Dae Sasitorn of www.lastrefuge.co.uk, who shot the
picture of the Uffington White Horse on page 37, fully
visible only from the air.

HALF TITLE The Devil's Punchbowl is a dramatic complex of
downland coombes and dry valleys incised into the escarpment
immediately below the Ridgeway. The main hollow rejoices in
the name of Crowhole Bottom. The sinuous valley leads down to
the pretty hamlet of Letcombe Basset on the spring line, where
the Letcombe Brook was noted for its watercress beds, alas, now
closed down by modern health and safety regulations.

TITLE PAGE This is a mid-winter view westwards down the
Ridgeway as it crests Whitehorse Hill. On the right rise the
earthen ramparts of Uffington Castle. A substantial Iron

Age hillfort, the ramparts were originally topped with a wall
of sarsen stones which replaced an earlier timber palisade.
Excavations have revealed little beyond domestic artefacts,
although it is known that the fort was familiar to Roman
troops. Wayland's Smithy lies amid the knot of trees beside
the ancient trackway in the distance left of centre, while
Liddington Castle is just visible on the far horizon.

RIGHT Seen beside the Ridgeway near Tring: autumnal guelder
rose (*Viburnum opulus*) and old man's beard, or traveller's joy
(*Clematis vitalba*).

CONTENTS

INTRODUCTION

Most roads have a beginning and an end but the Ridgeway has neither: what is left of it, and it is a remarkable stretch for a road of such antiquity, starts nowhere and concludes in time rather than space.

J.R.L. Anderson, *The Oldest Road* (1975)

Running for nearly 90 miles across southern England, the Great Ridgeway is one of our most ancient cross-county routes, its origins lost in time. The present Ridgeway National Trail with which this book is concerned is but a convenient and well-defined segment of a web of prehistoric trackways that once criss-crossed the country. Where possible these routes followed the high ground to avoid the primeval forest, marshy river valleys and attendant difficulties and dangers which made travel impractical or impossible through the valleys. This was Neolithic England in the raw.

Around five thousand years ago the first farmers arrived in Britain and, with something to trade, had reason to travel rather than merely to hunt and gather. The occasional tracks, particularly on the chalk uplands of the south, became regularly frequented and the route now known as the Great Ridgeway can be identified stretching along a sequence of chalk escarpments linking the North Sea in Norfolk to the English Channel in the vicinity of Axmouth in Dorset. Evidence proves that Europeans were already sailors of sorts – how else could they have arrived from the Continent, even from Spain? Thus inland connections from convenient landfalls would have become well-used routes over time, certainly by the arrival of Bronze Age folk

a thousand years later. These upland trackways were the only roads until the Romans came.

The Ridgeway National Trail itself is a distinctive, self-contained part of the time-honoured Great Ridgeway, and leads for 87 miles across five counties in the heart of central southern England. It traverses a rich, primarily agricultural landscape where the line of the route has, for much of the way, been well-used for centuries. It is usually well-defined geographically, and readily accessible to a large population.

The conjectured continuation north-eastwards of the ancient Great Ridgeway has been identified as the Icknield Way for a further hundred odd miles before continuing as the Peddars Way – later a Roman Road – for a similar distance to the Norfolk Coast. This latter route is also an official National Trail like the Ridgeway.

To the south-west, however, the topography is a little more complex as the ancient line enters the extensive chalk uplands of Salisbury Plain, Cranborne Chase and the Dorset Downs, where chalk escarpments abound and there is no obvious direct line. The Ramblers' Association – bless them – has established an unofficial Wessex Ridgeway of some 140 miles through south-west Wiltshire and Dorset, continuing the Ridgeway to the sea, much of it doubtless along ancient tracks which would surely have fanned out to many different destinations over this beautiful downland landscape.

The concept of a National Trail along the Wiltshire and Berkshire Downs and the Chilterns was first suggested by the Government's Hobhouse Committee on National

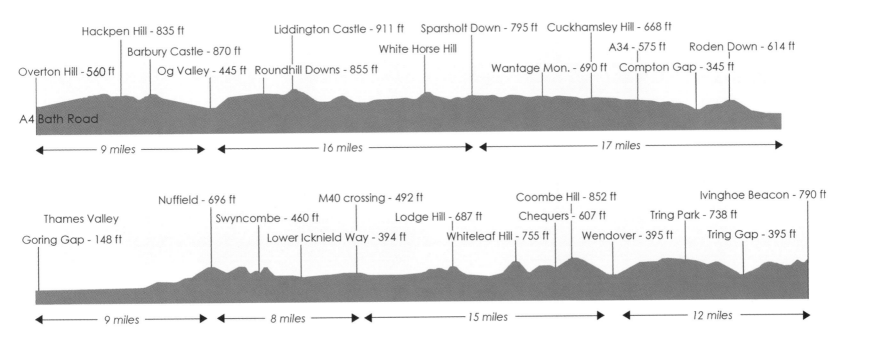

Overton Hill - 560 ft
Hackpen Hill - 835 ft
Barbury Castle - 870 ft
Og Valley - 445 ft
Liddington Castle - 911 ft
Roundhill Downs - 855 ft
White Horse Hill
Sparsholt Down - 795 ft
Wantage Mon. - 690 ft
Cuckhamsley Hill - 668 ft
A34 - 575 ft
Compton Gap - 345 ft
Roden Down - 614 ft

A4 Bath Road

← 9 miles → ← 16 miles → ← 17 miles →

Thames Valley
Goring Gap - 148 ft
Nuffield - 696 ft
Swyncombe - 460 ft
Lower Icknield Way - 394 ft
M40 crossing - 492 ft
Lodge Hill - 687 ft
Whiteleaf Hill - 755 ft
Coombe Hill - 852 ft
Chequers - 607 ft
Wendover - 395 ft
Tring Park - 738 ft
Tring Gap - 395 ft
Ivinghoe Beacon - 790 ft

← 9 miles → ← 8 miles → ← 15 miles → ← 12 miles →

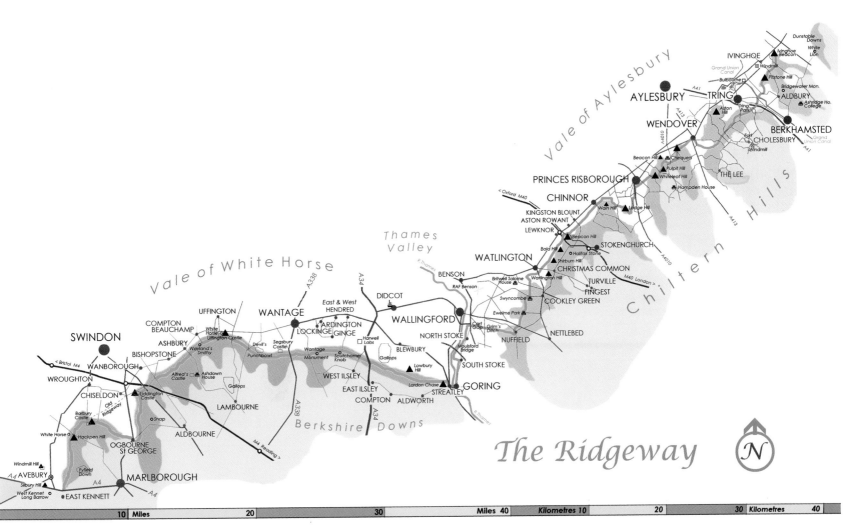

The Ridgeway

Parks as far back as 1947. But it was not until 1972 that the Government approved the route from Overton Hill near Marlborough to Ivinghoe Beacon near Dunstable, and it was opened as an official National Trail of 87 miles/139 km in September the following year at a ceremony held on Coombe Hill in the Chilterns.

The Ridgeway

Geographically the route is can be split equidistantly west and east of the River Thames, which cuts through the chalk escarpment at the Goring Gap. The well-defined green road west of the Gap, actually a fairly fragile chalk track and long a right-of-way, has been classed, ever since such things were first categorised, as a 'By-Way open to all Traffic'. Until comparatively recently, it was a favoured proving ground for the off-road motoring fraternity, both motorbikes and 4 x 4 vehicles, who left many stretches all but impassable on foot or on pushbike, particularly in winter.

Thankfully Natural England and the appropriate County Highway Authorities have now reclassified the western Ridgeway either as a bridleway or a restricted by-way, effectively closing most of it to motor vehicles. In places there are some seasonal exceptions and obviously neighbouring farmers have legitimate access to their land. Subsequently the surface has been repaired and in most places the going is now good for both pedestrians, equestrians and cyclists. On the virtually uninhabited high escarpment, regular watering points have been established for both man and animal.

Once east of the Thames, however, in the Chiltern Hills, the situation is slightly different. These hills are not bare, sparsely populated downland but are characteristically well-wooded, fairly well-peopled and liberally endowed with rights-of-way of all kinds. Here the Great Ridgeway, as such, was mostly a vague route along the hills, or in places, followed in summer the easier spring line at the foot of the escarpment. This was coincident with the Lower Icknield Way, which was probably originally of Roman origin.

Thus much of the route of the modern Ridgeway National Trail tends to be laced together from existing rights-of-way, enabling it to remain reasonably adjacent to the not-always-continuous edge. Although some bridle paths are included, for a large part the route is a footpath only. Sadly it is not possible to traverse the complete Chil-

tern section by bicycle or horseback as you can on the western Ridgeway.

However, as further west, the paths are properly maintained and there are regular waymarks, appropriate signposts and useful information boards. A Natural England Ridgeway Officer and his staff are responsible for the upkeep of the entire length of the National Trail, working from the Oxfordshire County Offices in close concert with the local authorities – of Wiltshire, Berkshire, Buckinghamshire and Hertfordshire – through whose territories the Ridgeway passes.

The Land

As we have already seen, most of the Ridgeway National Trail follows a chalk escarpment, laid down beneath the sea in late Cretaceous times between 65 and 100 million years ago. It has been estimated that it would have taken some 10,000 years to lay down 12in/30cm of chalk on the ocean floor.

The escarpment itself was formed around 30 million years ago by tectonic movements which pushed up the Alps and caused ripples across what is now southern England, at the same time as the land tilted towards the south-east. Subsequent erosion of this particular ripple has resulted in a steep scarp slope to the north-west and a gradual dip slope seamed with long valleys, such as that at Lambourne, to the south-east.

The highest point of the Ridgeway – Liddington Castle – reaches 910ft/277m, but the average altitude is nearer 650ft/200m, and rather less in the Chilterns, with the scarp slope falling steeply for around 250–300ft/75–90m before the angle eases.

Chalk is porous and although sculpted in earlier times by water, in our current dryer climate the drainage percolates underground leaving frequent, characteristic, dry valleys or coombes on both flanks of the escarpment. Some of these, incised into the scarp slope such as The Manger or Incombe Hole are, in a gentle way, quite spectacular.

In places the Cretaceous chalk was later covered by a thin layer of sandy sediment from ancient rivers, the so-called Reading Beds, which have long since been eroded away although they still remain deep below the London Basin. It is thought that water penetrating these beds deposited silica around the sand grains, forming chunks of

These signs on the Ridgeway at Berwick Bassett Down are self-explicit. Until recent years the track was frequently reduced to a quagmire in winter or wet weather.

harder sandstone within the soft sandy matrix. When the Reading Beds were eroded away these resistant chunks were left as sarsen boulders, a name which is thought to have been derived from 'Saracen' or 'foreigner'.

Sarsen stones are a notable feature of this Wessex chalk upland, particularly at its western end around Ashdown and on the Marlborough Downs where the stones scattered across the sheep country are known as Grey Wethers (a wether is a castrated ram), Druid Stones or Bridestones. The massive stones at Avebury, Stonehenge and Wayland's Smithy are sarsens, as are also the foundations and lower courses of many of the older buildings in the vales below the escarpment. East of the Thames there is a lesser-known Chiltern version of sarsen known as Denner Hill Stone which was used in the same way and is still exploited in a small quarry.

Later deposits of various kinds left patches of heavy, brown acid soil called clay-with-flints on the Chiltern chalk. Especially conducive for forest growth, this accounts for the prolific 'hanging' beech woods which cloak so much of the eastern Ridgeway.

Below the steep escarpment stretch the Vale of White Horse and the Vale of Aylesbury, essentially long, wide, flat valleys underlain by various clays and greensands. A feature of both vales is the line of ancient villages, and a little further back, small towns, established on the spring line along the foot of the escarpment. Water-cress beds still exist and were common on many of these clear chalk streams, while traditional local materials, such as sarsen, chalk blocks and flints, are seen in the older buildings, creating a very distinctive architectural heritage.

Only in five places are there breaches in the escarpment: the Ogbourne, Compton, Goring, Wendover and Tring Gaps. All were carved long ago by rivers flowing southwards at a time before the erosion of the clay vales, which were then more elevated than the chalk. Thus, but for local brooks, all but the valleys of the tiny River Og and the comparatively mighty Thames are now dry and fairly shallow.

Until Dr Beeching's railway closures, each was traversed by the 'iron horse', as are the three Chiltern gaps to this day. Only the impressive Goring Gap seriously impacts on the itinerary of the Ridgeway Trail. Having crossed the Thames at Goring, the official route follows the river's

The statue of King Alfred the Great dominates the Market Square at Wantage. Born here in 849 and succeeding his brother, King Ethelred I, as King of Wessex in 871, he defended England against the invading Danes for much of his life. He founded the navy, established a unified legal system and – it is said – burnt a lady's cakes. This statue was erected in 1877. Wantage, a pleasant, largely Georgian market town with a population of around 10,000 and just two miles below the Ridgeway, achieved borough status in 1177.

left bank for a while before striking across the now-wide Thames Valley and climbing once more onto the hills. Coming at mid-distance, this low-lying riverine section of the route provides an interesting contrast, a relief even, to the jaded Ridgeway traveller.

The Past

Trackway and Camp and Barrow lost,
Bare Downs where now is corn;
Old Wars, old Peace, old Arts that cease,
And so was England born!

Adapated, with apologies, from 'Puck's Song'
in Rudyard Kipling's *Puck of Pook's Hill* (1906)

We have a shrewd idea of the earliest origins of the Great Ridgeway. The New Stone Age people, who probably used it first, practised primitive agriculture. They lived fairly settled lives and constructed causewayed camps, probably as meeting places or cattle corrals rather than forts. The prime example is that on Windmill Hill just over 2 miles from Overton Down at the start of the Ridgeway. In the immediate vicinity they left many impressive remains, including the remarkable Avebury Stone Circle and the enigmatic Silbury Hill. They buried their important dead in long barrows, of which there are several beside the Ridgeway, and used flint tools, some of which must have been traded down the Great Ridgeway from the Norfolk flint mines.

The Beaker Folk who followed them – so called from the distinctive shape of their pottery – used bronze tools, cleared much of the forest and created the earliest field systems to survive in the vicinity of the Ridgeway. Their dead were buried in round barrows which feature in some number along the route, and it was these people who created the famous Uffington White Horse beside the Ridgeway – although for what purpose we cannot tell.

Around 700 BC settlers arrived who worked with iron. It was they who probably cleared what was left of the forest on the chalk uplands on which they ran sheep. They lived in villages and possibly built many of the linear earthworks such as Grim's Ditch which still exist on or around the Ridgeway. These were possibly to mark the boundaries of tribal areas or sub-kingdoms.

But their most impressive legacy is the chain of imposing hillforts that feature frequently along the Ridgeway. Timber stockades would have heightened the ramparts and some were even faced with sarsen stones, and there can be little doubt that they were defensive structures. The Great Ridgeway would have been a busy thoroughfare, one of many, and it seems likely that the downland then appeared little different from today, except that much is now under the plough, which has, alas, obliterated so many antiquities over the years.

Under the Romans, the way of life of the common people changed little; Pax Romana prevailed, commerce and no doubt general prosperity increased until the legions withdrew in 442. The Ridgeway would have been used locally of course, but the Romans engineered proper highways through the gaps in the chalk escarpment, such as the Og Valley and at Goring and Tring. They may also have built the Lower Icknield Way at the foot of the Chiltern scarp, which the National Trail now follows in several places.

In the so-called 'Dark Ages' which followed the departure of the legions, the Ridgeway once again became a major cross-country route as Roman order and infrastructure disintegrated. The hillforts were reoccupied to defend the upper Thames Valley as the Saxons arrived, gradually working their way down into Wessex. The convenient Ridgeway would have been used by both invading and defending armies, and in 556 the Saxons defeated the Romano-British defenders at the battle of Beranburgh – identified as Barbury Castle on the Ridgeway.

In due course Wessex became an Anglo-Saxon kingdom, indeed the very name Ridgeway is derived form the Anglo-Saxon *hryweg*, meaning 'high road'. Along with a network of other green lanes, it is mentioned in various existing land charters of the time, but in those days it would have been more of a route than a definitive road.

As part of Anglo-Saxon fortifications against the invading Danes, Alfred the Great established the little town of Wallingford as one of his chain of walled 'burhs'. The Ridgeway marked his defensive perimeter against their incursions from Oxford and the upper Thames Valley. Alfred eventually crushed the Danish host at the battle of Edington in 878, thought to have taken place on the northern lip of Salisbury Plain.

As a convenient track penetrating into the heart of Wessex and beyond, the Ridgeway would have been used by locals as an animal drove and by traders, pedlars, pilgrims and wayfarers of all descriptions. Nevertheless roads from town to town improved in medieval times and it lost its previous importance as a major east–west through-route.

In the late-sixteenth century, however, the first turn-pikes – toll roads – appeared, and until the coming of the railways the green lanes became busy with large herds of cattle and sheep as drovers herded their charges towards London and other large centres, avoiding the turnpike tolls. The Ridgway was no exception and was even a link in a drover's route from Wales.

From the earliest times the Ridgway had been a route, rather than a formal 'road' in the Roman sense: little more than a swath of hoof prints and wheels ruts along the downland crest. One can only imagine the result of the passage of thousands of cattle during a wet summer!

And so it remained until the Enclosure Acts of 1750–1800, which confirmed the boundaries of adjoining parishes and defined an exact course and width – ranging from 40 to 66 feet – for the Ridgeway. Thus it became an 'official' highway and was hedged and banked to restrain livestock from straying into the newly-arable fields alongside, and would have appeared not so very different from the trackway we know today.

The Route

For practical purposes the Ridgeway National Trail can be split into four, very different sections, each traversing a different landscape and enjoying a different atmosphere. It seems usual to travel from west to east, with the prevailing wind behind and advancing, as it were, through time, from Neolithic Avebury to the seventeenth-century Pitstone Windmill, but this is by no means compulsory.

Observations suggest that few people actually commit themselves to covering the 87 miles in a single expedition lasting probably a week. For those who do, several youth hostels, B&B accommodation and campsites exist in the villages below the escarpment, while unofficial trail-side bivouacs are an option for hardier souls.

The western Ridgeway offers magnificent rides for mountain bikers, but most serious pedestrians, on both east and west, seem to favour day trips, possibly completing the entire Ridgeway in instalments. Comparatively easy vehicle access, often via steep and narrow lanes, allow many folk to enjoy simple afternoon strolls.

The Marlborough Downs

Although starting officially on the A4 highway below Overton Down, those interested in prehistory will want to visit the nearby West Kennet Long Barrow, Silbury Hill, Avebury and the Grey Wethers on Fyfield Down before setting off. Essentially the Ridgeway follows a wide, undulating, flinty track along a downland crest exposed to the weather, wide views opening to the west and then to the north as the crest curves eastwards.

The trackway passes above the Hackpen White Horse, and after the only steep ascent, through the imposing Barbury Castle hillfort and its adjacent Country Park before following grassy Smeathe's Ridge down to Ogbourne St George, a total of just over 9 miles. Unfortunately motor vehicles are still permitted on the trackway in summer.

The White Horse Downs

After an initial steep climb and a section of frequently muddy farm track, the trail leads northwards, high above the Og Valley, 7 miles to Liddington Castle hillfort above Swindon. This superb vantage spot, at 909ft/277m the Ridgeway's highest point, requires a short diversion.

Now the route turns eastwards, marching along the well-defined escarpment for 26 miles to Streatley, the landscape changing almost imperceptibly. The main landmarks, in order and at convenient intervals, are Wayland's Smithy; Uffington Castle and the White Horse; the Devil's Punchbowl; Segsbury Castle hill-fort; the Baron Wantage Monument; Sutchamer Knob; the A34 tunnel, and Lowbury Hill, which requires another slight diversion. The Ridgeway itself is typically a broad grassy swath holding a narrower chalky or flinty surfaced track, but in places parallel ruts – the legacy of now-forbidden motor vehicles – challenge cyclists. There are only three stiff ascents, the steepest being the 160-foot/50m pull up to Uffington Castle.

While broad cornfields scattered with copses and shelter-belts characterise the surrounding landscape west of the A34 tunnel, eastwards the escarpment fades into wide rolling hills with frequent racehorse gallops until steeper ground falls away to the picturesque Goring Gap.

Bird's-eye views over the Vale are commonplace, but most feature the steaming cooling towers of Didcot Power Station somewhere in the wide panorama.

The Thames Valley

Georgian Streatley is little more than a pretty dormitory village, but just across the Thames bridge there are flesh-pots of sorts in more bustling Goring. This is boating country and Goring is known for its Thames weir and locks. A flat, easy footpath follows the left – eastern – riverbank upstream for 6 miles. Opposite the charming small town of Wallingford, which boasts a castle and all facilities, the route leaves the river to follow arrow-straight Grim's Ditch across the flat valley. After 4 miles and a bit of a climb the path reaches the little village of Nuffield on the ill-defined Chiltern crest.

The Chilterns

Now it's 34 miles to Ivinghoe and at first the route wanders along field paths, up and down through hilly country, pretty woods and a couple of gentleman's estates.

Descending to the Icknield Way, a hedged green road along the foot of the Chiltern escarpment, the Trail passes the interesting little town of Watlington, crosses beneath the M40 motorway and after 8 miles reaches Chinnor. Meanwhile at the top of the escarpment, Shirburn Hill, Bald Hill, Beacon Hill (790ft/240m) and Cowleaze Wood are

nature reserves displaying classic Chiltern chalk landform, superb views and, with luck, squadrons of reintroduced red kites performing aerobatics.

Once past Chinnor, more lowland field paths meander over wooded shoulders, over isolated little Lodge Hill and past Princes Risborough to Pulpit Hill, with its forest-cloaked hillfort. The path continues round the periphery of Chequers, the Prime Minister's secluded country retreat, before a steep ascent though fine beech woods gains imposing Coombe Hill (843ft/257m). After this rather vague section of eight miles, Coombe Hill, with its tall monument and wide panorama, is a major landmark.

Descending to Wendover and down its attractive High Street, the path climbs again into the hills, but now through woods and fields well back from the northern slopes. It passes along the boundary of Tring Park on the wooded escarpment edge once more, and drops into the Tring Gap.

Here the A41, the Grand Union Canal and the main railway are all crossed before the final, downland massif rears ahead. A gradual ascent leads to bare Pitstone Hill and more steeply to Steps Hill, where deep coombs and steep hillsides define the now impressive escarpment. A final, steep, chalky climb reaches the wind-blown and isolated Ivinghoe Beacon (764ft/233m), with its much-denuded hillfort, the official terminus of the Ridgeway National Trail.

In late summer elderberries (*Sambucus nigra*) hang in profusion beside the Ridgeway, particularly along the eastern section of the Berkshire Downs.

Blackberries (or brambles – *Rubus fruticosus*). In season blackberry pickers frequent the Ridgeway in some numbers, but rarely far from the motorable lanes which reach it every few miles.

MARLBOROUGH DOWNS

Enigmatic Silbury Hill, seen here from the south east across the meadows beside the infant River Kennet, is a major feature in the Neolithic landscape which marks the start of the Ridgeway, just 2 miles to the east. Standing beside the A4 (the old Bath Road, originally a Roman highway), its purpose has perplexed travellers and archaeologists throughout the centuries. John Aubrey wrote that it was said to be the burial mound of a King Sil who was 'buried here on horseback and the hill raysed while a posset of milke was seething', but only a broken deer antler pick has ever been found. It is the largest man-made mound in Europe, standing 130 ft/39m high with its base covering over 5 acres.

ABOVE Early morning at the high point of the Avenue, with the tower of Avebury church appearing below. A double row of sarsen megaliths, the Avenue extends for half a mile south-east from the Avebury Circle, though it originally led the whole way to the Sanctuary, another complex of stone circles which were destroyed in 1724 by the local farmer. The Ridgeway Trail starts across the A4 immediately opposite the Sanctuary.

RIGHT An eerie winter morning in the Stone Circle at Avebury. Built some 4,000 years ago and obviously a monument of great religious or ritual significance, it was described by Aubrey in 1663 as 'a monument which does as much excel Stonehenge as a cathedral does a parish church'.

The circle is enormous and is enclosed by a once-high earthen bank over three quarters of a mile in circumference and encompassing 29 acres, while two subsidiary inner circles and a later village stand in its centre. The main circle originally comprised about 100 huge sarsen stones, the highest 21ft/6.5m tall and each weighing at least 50 tons, but it seems that there may have been over 600 stones in the entire complex. Alas, fewer than fifty now remain, most having been broken up for building stone over the centuries.

During excavations in 1939 an intriguing skeleton was discovered beneath one of the fallen stones, dated to the fourteenth century. From the instruments he carried it seems that he was a barber-surgeon. Did the stone fall on him or is the story more mysterious?

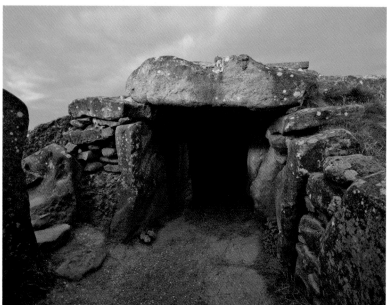

ABOVE Another important feature in this remarkable Neolithic landscape is the impressive West Kennet Long Barrow. The largest of its kind in England, it crouches on a downland spur above the infant Kennet, just a mile from the start of the Ridgeway. The sarsen-built tomb may be 5,000 years old, and consists of two pairs of burial chambers either side of a long passage with a further chamber at the end. It seems to have been in use for a thousand years or so and the remains of forty-six people have been uncovered during excavations. As the picture shows, it is a moody place.

LEFT Is this the entrance to the Underworld? The portals of the West Kennet Long Barrow.

After less than 2 miles, the Ridgeway crosses an ancient green lane ascending from Avebury. This is the Herepath (Old English for 'military marching track') and it continues over a low crest and a racehorse gallop to Fyfield Down National Nature Reserve, a landscape little changed over two millennia. The down is scattered with stunted hawthorns, gorse bushes and thousands of 'Grey Wethers' sarsens, among which wandering real sheep echo their nickname. The origin of these strange boulders is described on page 10. Fyfield Down is a beautiful place, well worth the short diversion.

ABOVE Grey Wethers were once scattered all over the Downs but through the centuries, many have been taken for building stone or removed by farmers. This massive sarsen boulder still lies on Monkton Down high above Winterbourne Monkton and a few yards west of the Ridgeway Trail.

RIGHT ABOVE A misty morning beside the Ridgeway on Avebury Down – beech clumps like these are characteristic of the chalk downland over which the Ridgeway passes.

RIGHT BELOW A typical view from the Ridgway in early spring; ridge after ridge fading away into the evening mist.

FAR LEFT The White Horse of Hackpen is one of Wiltshire's famous chalk figures. Carved into the north-west flank of Hackpen Hill, it is invisible from the Ridgeway which runs a few yards above. Here it is seen over the minor road leading from Broad Hinton at the foot of the escarpment over to Marlborough; a convenient parking place is situated at the top of the steep hill where it crosses the Ridgeway. This particular horse was created in 1838 by the Parish Clerk and village publican of Broad Hinton to celebrate the Coronation of Queen Victoria.

LEFT ABOVE First signs of spring in a beech clump beside the Ridgeway near Hackpen Hill

LEFT BELOW Morning mist clears over Barbury Castle as the Ridgway approaches this imposing hillfort. From the saddle immediately below its steep slopes, the original Ridgeway descends across the northern flank of the hill to make a beeline over the vale to Chiseldon and the northern slopes of Liddington Castle beyond. Much of this route is now part of the modern road network and the National Trail has been routed along a more attractive, if rather longer, sequence of tracks. The ascent of Barbury Castle (870ft/265m) is steep but short.

Sheep graze along the southern ramparts of Barbury Castle. Still impressive, the double row of ramparts and ditches enclose an area of nearly 12 acres where excavations have unearthed jewellery and chariot fittings besides the expected hut circles and storage pits. Originally a hillfort dating from the IronAge, it was re-fortified after the Romans left and was the site of a crucial battle in AD 556 when Cynric and his invading Saxons beat the defending Britons. Barbury is a corruption of Bera Byrg meaning Bera's Hill. The distant beech clumps stand on Preshute Down (883ft/269m) beside the Ridgeway.

Rooks nest in the beeches ranged along the escarpment lip beside Barbury Castle. Plaques on sarsen boulders near by commemorate the local countryside writers Richard Jefferies (1848–87) and Alfred Williams (1877–1930), while shallow ditches mark the site of a deserted medieval village. The whole area was established a Country Park in 1972 and there is a car park, a little café and a campsite close to the lane leading up from the north.

LEFT On descending into the Og Valley, the first buildings one comes to in Ogbourne St George are the church and adjacent manor, in a tranquil setting beside the little Og Brooks. A priory built by the Norman Abbey of Bec, which held the land, once stood beside the thirteenth-century church, while the Manor House is Jacobean and bears the date of 1619. Ogbourne was Occa's burn or stream. A diversion through the hamlet of Southend avoids the long village altogether.

ABOVE This tomb, one of several of similar vintage in the churchyard, dates to March 1786

WHITE HORSE DOWNS

BELOW A 'blackthorn winter' on the Ridgeway. It's actually late March on the muddy green lane along the escarpment edge on Roundhill Downs, high above the Og Valley. Leading northwards towards Liddington Castle, this is the National Trail diversion from the old Ridgeway and as elsewhere, it doubles as a farm track.

RIGHT Blackthorn (sloe, or *Prunus spinosa*) on the Ridgeway. These hedges have been here at least since the late eighteenth century, and probably long before that.

LEFT This is the view westwards from the Ridgeway on Upham Down, over the now-wide Og Valley, towards the northern shoulder of the Marlborough Downs and Barbury Castle. The strategic position of the hillfort is evident. Both the A346 – originally a Roman highway – and an old railway line, now an excellent cycle track – run from Marlborough to Swindon, left to right across the centre of the picture.

ABOVE On Whitefield Hill above the Og Valley, the Ridgeway is bordered by a narrow strip of woodland for a mile or so, possibly the remains of an ancient hedge. To avoid the muddy farm track, a parallel footpath has been established through the gnarled oaks and stunted beeches, and in a few weeks time bluebells will carpet the banks.

On a spur just half a mile off the Ridgeway is the site of the deserted medieval village of Upham, cleared to make way for sheep. John of Gaunt hunted here and the original manor house was a favourite haunt of his. The present manor, Upham Court (built in 1599), and the nearby farm still exist as the hamlet of Upper Upham.

In the deep dry valley below once stood the village of Snap, of which little remains but mounds and banks, what must have been a pond, a very ancient walnut tree, a derelict, rust-eaten windpump and an overgrown green lane. The village, first mentioned in documents in 1377, died gradually as the wells dried up and the last few cottages were abandoned in 1913, apparently after a rich Ramsbury butcher purchased the valley as cattle pasture. A current Upham resident tells that the shade of an angry Granny Fisher stalks the site at night but by day it is 'a rabbit heaven'.

ABOVE LEFT A cyclist takles the stony lane leading down to Snap from the hamlet of Upper Upham.

ABOVE CENTRE Inscribed 'In Memory of the People of Snap. Toothill School 5-8-1991', this poignant stone stands on the site of the deserted village.

ABOVE RIGHT The sweet nuts from this ancient walnut tree must once have been prized by a Snap cottage family.

BELOW Sleek cattle graze at the site of Snap village, whose mounds and probable pond are seen below. The Ridgeway crosses the downs above.

RIGHT Ripening corn and blackthorn hedges border the Ridgeway as it heads north over Upham Down towards Liddington Castle. This 4-mile stretch of the route is relatively unfrequented.

LEFT The Ridgeway is well signed, as this late-summer picture at its junction with the ancient Sugar Way drove on Upham Down demonstrates.

ABOVE Wayfarers share the Ridgeway with wildlife of all sorts – these small snails are characteristic of the chalk downs.

RIGHT The ridge narrows as the climb up to Liddington Castle – just out of sight over the crest – begins. There are wide views to west and east where the parallel escarpment of Sugar Hill above Aldbourne is a dominant feature.

OPPOSITE, ABOVE Echoing Barbury Castle, just 4 miles south-westwards across the vale, Liddington Castle and its conspicuous earthwork ramparts beckon approaching travellers along the Ridgeway.

The highest point on the Ridgeway, the hillfort of Liddington Castle reaches 911ft/277m. It stands above the meeting point of four counties – Wiltshire, Oxfordshire, Berkshire and Gloucestershire – and is visible for miles around, even from the Chilterns on a clear day. Beneath its steep northern slopes lie the noisy M4 motorway and the burgeoning Swindon conurbation. The castle is just 300 yards off the Ridgeway, reached by a permissive path.

Once known as Badbury Castle – Liddington is a nearby village – the still-formidable double ramparts were once faced with sarsen stones, while the deep single ditch encloses an area of almost 8 acres. The *Anglo-Saxon Chronicle* suggests that the Battle of Mons Badonicus was fought here at some date around AD 516 when Romano-British troops under a leader called Arthur (who may have been the legendary king) defeated the invading Saxons, checking their advance into Wessex for a further half-century.

The area is certainly strategic, for the nearby village of Wanborough stands on Ermin Street and very close to both the Roman road from Marlborough and the Ridgeway. It is said to have been the place where the Saxon warlord Cedric defeated his uncle Ceawlin in AD 591 and where a century later King Ine confronted the encroaching Mercians. It all sounds quite feasible.

OPPOSITE, BELOW Sheep graze the still-imposing ramparts of Liddington Castle. Barbury Castle, the hillfort on the northern escarpment of the Marlborough Downs, is seen in the distance.

BELOW In more recent times, Liddington Castle was an especially inspirational spot for Richard Jefferies, the celebrated Victorian naturalist and writer, who was born at its foot. This memorial plaque graces the toposcope beside the OS trig point.

LEFT Silhouetted against a fiery dusk, the landmark beech clump on Liddington Hill is seen from the east. The hillfort itself is invisible from this direction, but lies a short way beyond the trees.

ABOVE Just a mile and a half off the Ridgeway, in a dry valley leading down eventually to the racing-stables village of Lambourne, stands Ashdown House. Seen here from the west, the house was built after the Restoration by the Earl of Craven as a fanciful hunting lodge, and stands in an extensive park to which there is free access. 'A perfect doll's house,' according to Pevsner, it is now a National Trust property.

Alfred's Castle close by is a small hillfort and may be the place where the Anglo-Saxon forces under King Ethelred I and his brother Alfred (later 'The Great') gathered before defeating the Danes at the bloody Battle of Ashdown in 871. Along the edge of the park, opposite steep Kingstone Down, is another great scattering of sarsen boulders.

The attractive village of Ashbury, one of the Ridgeway's characteristic spring-line villages, stands just below the escarpment less than a mile off the route. The older cottages are thatched and constructed of chalk blocks on a sarsen foundation, and there are two water mills, neither now in working order.

Compton Beauchamp is the next hamlet to Ashbury below the escarpment. Today there is little here besides the moated Compton House and the tiny, thirteenth-century chalkstone church of St Swithun, which boasts both medieval and contrasting modern stained glass, and which is seen here on a crisp winter day.

Atmospheric, even eerie, Wayland's Smithy stands beside the Ridgeway above Compton Beauchamp. Fronted by four massif sarsens, it is a Neolithic long barrow or chambered tomb, dated by radio-carbon to around 2850 BC, superimposed on an earlier version. Excavations revealed a total of twenty-two skeletons from the two periods. In Saxon mythology Wayland was the Smith to the Gods, and he was said to shoe your horse overnight if you tethered it beside the barrow with an appropriate payment. As far as I know, this generous offer has not been recently tested.

In due course Whitehorse Hill, crowned by the earthworks of Uffington Castle, rears ahead. Now well back from the escarpment edge, the trackway tackles the hill head-on, the final steep section exposing naked, white chalk. It was not always thus as the older picture shows, shot in the same place in 1982 before motor vehicles were forbidden. Bless the Ridgeway Officer and his team!

RIGHT, ABOVE On a late December afternoon, the Vale of White Horse lies spread out below in this view from the ramparts of Uffington Castle, at 858ft/261m the highest point for miles around. Uffington village can be made out in the distance, on the right.

RIGHT, BELOW The famous White Horse of Uffington can be seen properly only from the air, in this case from slightly west of north over the coombe of the Manger. This aerial picture by Dae Sasitorn explains the relationship of the White Horse to Uffington Castle hillfort and to the Ridgeway, the white chalk trackway extending diagonally across the top of the picture. Dragon Hill is the small rounded tump at lower left.

FAR RIGHT The Manger hangs on the northern flak of the escarpment almost below the muzzle of the White Horse. It is a deep coombe or dry valley sculpted by surface drainage, probably melt water during or soon after the Ice Age. Little, bare, flat-topped Dragon Hill nearby, an outlier of the escarpment, is so-called because St George allegedly slew his dragon there and its tainted blood has blighted the grass ever since.

A cyclist descends the Ridgeway eastwards from Whitehorse Hill en route to Kingstonhill Barn above Kingston Lisle – the next junction with a metalled lane. In the distance, some 12 miles away across Vale of White Horse, stands the Didcot Power Station, a landmark visible from almost the entire length of the Ridgeway. The Chiltern escarpment can be made out along the far horizon.

Standing just back from the spring line, Uffington is one of the larger villages at the foot of the downs. Besides an interesting thirteenth-century church, Uffington is notable for Tom Brown, or at least for Thomas Hughes, the author of *Tom Brown's Schooldays* who was born here in 1822 and grew up in the village. Doubtless he learnt the three Rs in the old single-room school house beside the church, built of chalkstone in 1617, and now the Tom Brown Museum.

LEFT These strip lynchets are cut into the steep hillside below the Ridgeway at Britchcombe, between Uffington Castle and Kingston Lisle village. Archaeologists consider that such cultivation terraces were made at some date between Anglo-Saxon times, when ploughs first became strong enough to work such hard hillsides, and the Napoleonic Wars, but always when there were shortages of arable land elsewhere.

ABOVE A summery view looking westwards along the Ridgeway as it descends Sparsholt Down. Hillbarn Clump (742ft/226m) is seen on the far skyline.

LEFT It is soon after dawn at the tumulus near Pewit Farm on Lattin Down. The Baron Wantage Monument is visible in the far distance.

BELOW The Ridgeway approaches the Baron Wantage Monument on Betterton Down on an early morning in September. It is certainly a notable landmark.

The tall column of the Baron Wantage Monument stands beside the Ridgeway. Born in 1834, Lord Wantage was the local magnate and a war hero. The inscription reads:

Robert Loyd Lindsay Baron Wantage VC KCB 1901.
Inkerman 1854 Alma 1854.
This cross is raised in his memory by his wife.
My help cometh from the Lord who made Heaven and Earth. I will lift up mine eyes unto the Hills from whence cometh my help.
IN OBIT V PAX POST OBIT V M SAINS POST TENEBRAS. LVX. IN LUCE SPES

Which says it all.

With the Baron Wantage Monument still visible on the western skyline, the Ridgeway crosses Ridgeway Down above the little Lockinge Valley. These narrow ruts, cut by motor vehicles in the past, can demand precision riding from cyclists. The landscape hereabout owes much to Lord Wantage, who planted hundreds of trees in clumps, copses and shelter-belts.

A surprise awaits passers-by should they take a glimpse through the iron gates of Betterton House at East Lockinge. The House occupies the site of the deserted medieval village of Betterton. East Lockinge, a model village created around 1860 by Lord Wantage, is another of those pretty villages on the spring line below the escarpment, a short distance from the Ridgeway.

East Lockinge parish church stands beside the Betterton Brook, a picturesque chalk stream and a fishing preserve. Little now remains of Lord Wantage's mansion which stood near by.

LEFT This is the track to Ardington Mill, just a short way down the stream from the two adjacent Lockinge villages. It is a most attractive little valley.

BELOW At Ardington, the Betterton Brook gains a tributary and becomes the Ardington Brook, to join the Thames in due course near Abingdon. It is a well-known fly-fishing stream. Lord Wantage's parkland stretches beyond.

ABOVE The hamlets of East and West Ginge nestle in the narrow valley of the Ginge Brook which parallels that of the Betterton Brook. Beyond the lush paddocks, East Ginge House is just visible in the trees, with Ardington Down and the long line of the chalk escarpment in the distance.

RIGHT The Ridgeway runs along the crest of Cuckhamsley Hill (668ft/203m), seen here from near East Ginge, the tiny chalk-stream hamlet at its foot.

At its summit beside the trackway a curious croissant-shaped mound known as Scutchamer Knob stands in a straggly, fly-tipped copse. Possibly a Neolithic barrow remodelled later as a Saxon meeting place, it may even be the burial place of the Saxon chieftain Cwicchelm, from whom the hill itself is possibly named. It is mentioned in the *Anglo-Saxon Chronicle*, which describes an engagement with the Danes in 1006, who having burnt Wallingford, advanced along the Ridgeway to 'Cuckhamsley Knob' and vanquished the local levies.

The charming little medieval church of Holy Trinity at West Hendred sits in the narrow valley bottom of the Ginge Brook. Among other graffiti in the porch is the date 1671 scratched by some idle hand. Adjoining and much larger, East Hendred became extremely prosperous in the Middle Ages, with a market charter and a regular cloth fair.

LEFT Dusk on the Ridgeway on Cuckhamsley Hill. Up here the flinty track runs along a wide green road lined with odd hawthorn bushes, probably all that remain of long-neglected, late-eighteenth-century hedges.

ABOVE Hawthorn berries (*Crataegus monogyna*) on Chilton Downs. Hawthorn is another autumnal fruit found in great abundance along the Ridgeway. The line of trees in the middle distance actually masks the modern A34 trunk road as it descends steeply from the escarpment, while the landmark cooling towers of Didcot Power Station loom on the horizon. Dubbed rather incongruously 'The Cathedral of the Vale', the massive power station opened in 1968. Its main chimney is 650ft/128m tall and, with six cooling towers topping 325ft/100m, it is no surprise that it is visible from afar, as we shall see.

LEFT On Gore Hill the Ridgeway passes beneath the A34 Newbury–Oxford trunk road in a concrete tunnel which the Compton Art Group has decorated with charming vernacular murals depicting the local villages. With a minor road head near by, it is not surprising that the murals have been needlessly defaced by thoughtless vandals.

BELOW On Gore Hill two cyclists set off towards Compton Downs. The chalk escarpment is fading now into wide, rolling uplands, scattered with racehorse gallops. Streatley is just 8 miles distant.

This is the pond at East Ilsley – 'Market Ilsley' – a village once boasting thirteen pubs just a mile south of the Ridgeway. Until 1934, a busy fortnightly agricultural market was held here, while at the annual sheep fair, second only to Smithfield, as many as 80,000 sheep might change hands in a single day, with drovers driving their flocks over the downs from as far away as Salisbury.

There is little habitation on the Berkshire Downs and no natural water. In conjunction with local farmers, the Ridgeway authorities have installed water points for man and horse at intervals along the route. This one, accompanied by a small brass plaque in memory of a Dr Basil Philips, a local GP, who presumably sponsored it, stands on Compton Downs above East Ilsley.

In fairly remote country now, the Ridgeway descends from Compton Downs towards the so-called Compton Gap. At one time the railway linking Newbury to Didcot and Oxford ran through this shallow dry valley, and the route crosses the old railway cutting on a bridge close to the long-gone Blewbury Halt. On the right skyline rises Lowbury Hill with the Ridgeway traversing its foot above the ploughed hillside. In the centre the Fairmile green lane leads over the crest.

Poppies ripple across this field beside the Ridgeway on Roden Down above Compton. The line of bushes in the mid-distance marks the Ridgeway leading from the conspicuous clump of trees (around OS spot height 146m). The gallops on Blewbury and Compton Downs are seen in the distance and the tower of Chilton church on the horizon, far right.

Crowned by a trig point memorial, an ancient tumulus and the foundations of a Roman temple, Lowbury Hill at 612ft/186m is a major landmark in this wide, rolling landscape. There is local evidence that the hill was a battlefield where King Ethelred fought the Danes. This view from the hillside is westwards to where the Ridgeway, visible in the centre distance, descends Blewbury Down. It passes through the nearer clump of trees (OS spot height 146m) to follow the hedge-line below the corn stubble, left.

LEFT The Church of St Mary at Aldworth stands just a mile and a half south of the Ridgeway and dates to the early fourteenth century. Besides the thousand-year-old yew tree outside, the church is famed for the 'Aldworth Giants' inside. These are eight remarkable stone effigies, six of the local de la Beche family and all unfortunately rather hacked about by seventeenth-century Puritans

ABOVE One of the Aldworth Giants – this one is Sir Philip de la Beche II, gentleman-valet to Edward II, son of Sir Philip and Lady Joan, who was imprisoned in Scarborough Castle in 1322, pardoned by Edward III in 1327, and appointed High Sheriff of Berkshire and Oxfordshire in 1332. Obviously quite a fellow.

Although it has already gradually lost height, it is almost without warning that the Ridgeway falls away off the rolling downs into the great coombe of Streatley Warren, a characteristic dry valley now leading down eastwards into the Goring Gap. The valley is actually some 2½ miles long and much of it is under the plough, but the area is very popular with hikers and strollers of all descriptions because several cottages, a farm and a small car park are situated at a metalled road head half way up the coombe. In autumn the high hedges are heavy with berries of all kinds.

OPPOSITE Lardon Chase is a downland shoulder, the final fling of the Berkshire Downs before they fall to the Goring Gap. Together with Lough Down on the far side of the hedge, Lardon Chase forms the southern containing arm of the Streatley Warren coombe and thus rises immediately above the Ridgeway as it approaches Streatley. It is a splendid viewpoint, looking down from a height of 455ft/138m on Streatley and the Ridgeway crossing of the Thames, and it is a National Trust property. This is a view in early May along the shoulder towards the Chiltern escarpment rising on the far side of the Goring Gap.

BELOW On the far right is Streatley High Street, with the prominent fifteenth-century tower of St Mary's church rising near by. The Thames is best seen to the left of centre while Goring village extends over the far bank with the Chiltern escarpment forming the horizon.

LEFT A swan glides over a tranquil Thames backwater in the Streatley water meadows.

Streatley and Goring, the former in Berkshire the latter in Oxfordshire, are linked by twin bridges over a midstream eyot (island), but until 1838 the only way across the Thames was by ferry or ford. Such a ford must have existed since the earliest times when the meandering river was wide and shallow here with shelving, gravelly banks. But methods of crossing were dangerous and unreliable – in 1674 alone fifty people were drowned – and the nearest bridge was at Wallingford five miles upstream; nevertheless the first bridge here was not built until 1838.

Today Goring boasts a pound lock, one of forty-five on the non-tidal Thames, and one of the forty-eight weirs which control its water level. Its fame as a centre for pleasure boating is perhaps epitomised by Jerome K. Jerome's Edwardian novel *Three Men in a Boat* – in which the three men enjoyed a lunch at the Bull Inn in Streatley, which still stands beside the Ridgeway National Trail as it enters the village.

RIGHT ABOVE A spring evening beside the Thames at Goring. The lock lies to the left of the lock keeper's cottage and the weir is to the right.

RIGHT BELOW Early summer on the Thames at Goring Lock. A clump of kingcups (or marsh marigold, *Caltha palustris*), of which there are many hereabouts, graces the Streatley water meadows.

ABOVE An evening view downstream from Goring Bridge. The steep wooded slopes on the right rise above Streatley to the Berkshire Downs.

LEFT An evening view in the opposite direction – upstream – from Goring Bridge. The Ridgeway crosses the bridge and continues along the eastern or true left bank, to South and North Stoke and the bridge at Wallingford.

The pretty village of South Stoke stands just back from the Thames a mile and a half above Goring. There used to be a small ferry here across the river to Moulsford and the green tunnel of Ferry Lane leads from the village down to the river bank. Both the lane and the ferry lie on the ancient Icknield Way.

RIGHT A coot (*Fulica atra*) goes about its business on a secluded backwater pool in the reed beds beside Ferry Lane.

This is a typical riverbank scene on this part of the Thames. A residential narrowboat is moored beside the Ridgeway path opposite Moulsford where a boat yard displays a fleet of smart motor cruisers for hire. Next door a neat lawn and weeping willows suggest a probably salubrious private residence.

OPPOSITE In this view across from the National Trail, the far bank is occupied by lawns and willows, with Moulsford's little church set back in the trees.

A London-bound express sweeps over Brunel's famous Moulsford Bridge, known locally as 'The Four Arches'. The bridge crosses the river at an angle with the four 62ft/19m arches ranged obliquely and the bricks laid askew – Brunel was very ingenious. Built for the Great Western Railway's main line to Bath and Bristol, the bridge was completed in 1839 and widened with a parallel span in 1892, though to a quality rather less than Brunel's original design and workmanship.

RIGHT A pleasure barge sailing downstream shoots Brunel's Moulsford Bridge.

Immediately upstream from the bridge the river widens and here there are three small eyots which are supposedly haunted. Long ago there was a mill here and a 'flash lock' – a hazardous early form of lock that was effectively a weir with a single gate.

ABOVE The Ridgeway is seen here near Littlestoke Manor while a 'gin-palace' motor-cruiser proceeds downstream towards Goring. The Trail follows the river bank closely for 2 miles between South and North Stoke.

RIGHT Teasels (*Dipsacus fullonum*) stand beside the Trail as it approaches North Stoke, the Chilterns rising in the distance. Here the path diverges a little way from the river bank. The fields in between Goring and Mongewell tend to be huge and hedgeless, bounded only by roads, a hangover from the medieval open field system which remained extant in these parishes until they were eventually enclosed only in the mid-nineteenth century.

Built to command the adjacent river crossing, not much of Wallingford Castle remains standing. After the wars of Stephen and Matilda, the Treaty of Wallingford was signed here in 1154 giving the throne to Henry II. Later the castle became a favoured residence of Henry III but in the Civil War, Wallingford was the last Royalist stronghold to surrender and the victorious Parliamentarians blew it up. It has been a ruin ever since.

Wallingford was established as one of King Alfred's fortified 'burhs' defending Wessex against the Danes, and some of his earthen ramparts still survive. The town was an Anglo-Saxon river port with a market and its own mint. Today it is an attractive, largely Georgian little town boasting a 1670 Town Hall overlooking a central market square. Naturally it can offer most facilities.

All told there are seventeen arches to Wallingford Bridge but only three of the original medieval ones survive, for the bridge was rebuilt in 1751 and again in 1809. This was a very important river crossing before bridges were built at Abingdon and Goring.

Having turned away from the river opposite Wallingford, the Ridgeway Trail sets off across the flatlands of the Thames Valley towards the Chilterns, following the Iron Age earthwork of Grim's Ditch for over 3 miles. Grim's Ditch, which extends now intermittently across the Chilterns, is something of an enigma, and is currently thought to have been a land boundary between tribes or petty kingdoms. 'Grim' was another appellation for the Norse god Odin, whose name the Anglo-Saxons lent to many puzzling linear earthworks. This picture shows the footpath crossing Cart Gap where a minor lane breaches Grim's Ditch, which here consists of two raised and thickly hedged banks with a ditch in between and was obviously impassable to wheeled vehicles.

Red kites soar over Nuffield Hill, almost 700ft/200m above sea level. Grim's Ditch and the Ridgeway ascend Morrell's Bottom, the little valley beyond the fields, to gain the heights of the Chiltern Hills at Nuffield. Beyond stretches the Thames Valley with the long escarpment of the Berkshire Downs lying across the far horizon.

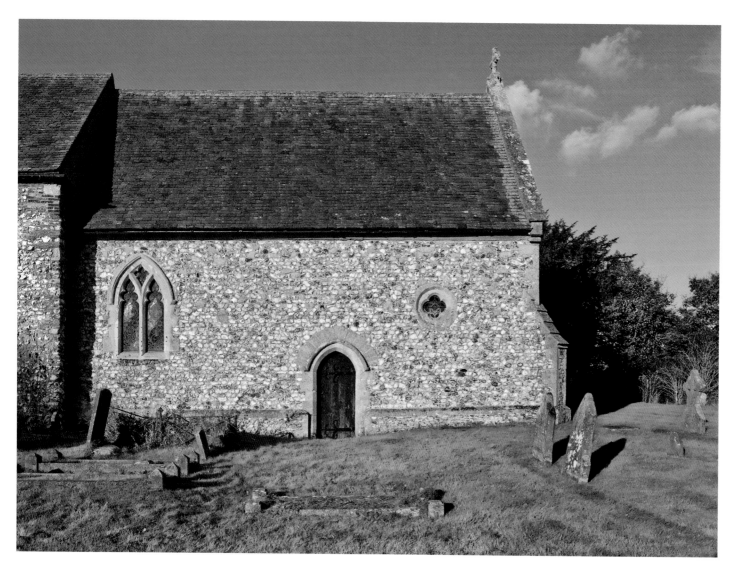

This is the chancel of little, characteristically flint-walled, parish church of Holy Trinity at Nuffield. It is said to date from the seventh century but most of it is some 500 years younger and it boasts a Norman font. The vicar has kindly placed a notice inviting Ridgeway travellers to refresh themselves at the water tap in the churchyard.

LEFT In the churchyard lies the grave of Lord Nuffield – the erstwhile William Morris, industrialist, philanthropist and founder of the Morris Motor Company, later the Nuffield Group and ultimately British Leyland. Leaving school at fifteen, he opened a bicycle shop in Oxford a year later and in due course began repairing early motor vehicles. He opened a garage, prospered, founded Morris Motors and started manufacturing cars. His first, highly successful product was the famous 'Bull Nose' Morris of 1912, and it can be said that he bought the motor car within the reach of everyman. A rich and generous benefactor, he gave away as much money as he made.

The Didcot Power Station, some 10 miles distant, is still a constant companion. This is the view due west over the Thames Valley from the Ridgeway at Ewelme Park on the rumpled western edge of the Chilterns.

Ewelme Park is a beautifully kept gentleman's estate-cum-model farm. From the well-signposted Ridgeway path, there are only glimpses of the mansion, a replica of the original Elizabethan manor house which was destroyed by fire in 1913. A few yards further on the path passes these lovely farm buildings of brick and flint, time-honoured Chiltern building materials.

As it leaves Ewelme Park, the Ridgeway proceeds down this beech avenue and into open fields before descending into the Swyncombe Estate though a wood with the intriguing name of Jacob's Tent.

ABOVE The bluebell (*Endymion nonscriptus*) is a characteristic British flower and when it blooms in spring, it becomes one of the glories of the Chiltern Hills. This is a bluebell-carpeted ride crossed by a right-of-way footpath in Haycroft Wood, a short distance off the Ridgeway above the Swyncombe Valley.

RIGHT Swyncombe House is glimpsed through the trees on the edge of Straights Plantation on the hillside a few yards off the Ridgeway. The house, standing in fine parkland at the head of the coombe, is an 1840s replacement of an earlier, probably Elizabethan, mansion destroyed by fire. Like Ogbourne St George, Swyncombe manor was once a holding of Bec Abbey in Normandy.

ABOVE Sheep have been run on the Chiltern Hills from the earliest times, although in recent centuries, beech woods have curtailed the extent of the pasture land. Contented-looking spring lambs and their mothers graze on the flanks of Colliers Hill on the Swyncombe estate.

LEFT This old track down Colliers Bottom on the Swyncombe estate is known as Ladies Walk and it leads eventually to Ewelme village. Having joined it below Jacob's Tent, the Ridgeway continues along Ladies Walk up the coombe to the little Swyncombe church.

Continuing along Ladies Walk, the Ridgeway passes though an avenue of huge horse-chestnut trees behind Swyncombe House.

Serving no obvious community save that connected to the big house, the charming church of St Botolph at Swyncombe belies its tiny exterior and appears surprisingly roomy inside. Built soon after the Norman Conquest from local flints set in an unusual herringbone-pattern, it features an uncommon semi-spherical apse and its bells date to the thirteenth and fourteenth centuries. It was restored fairly benignly soon after the nearby mansion was rebuilt in the 1840s. A Snowdrop Festival is held at the church each February.

Britwell Salome House is a picturesque Palladian villa just visible from the Ridgeway before it descends to join the Icknield Way near North Farm. It was built in 1728 for Sir Edward Simeon who added the pineapple-topped column on the lawn in 1764 as a memorial to his parents. The house incorporated a discreet chapel as the family were recusant Catholics, and there is evidence that a secret underground passage was incorporated to provide an escape route for a proscribed priest in an emergency. This is the south-eastern aspect of the house.

The Ridgeway touches the outskirts of little Watlington, with its narrow Georgian streets and striking Town Hall built in 1665. Originally the upper story was the Grammar School and the lower the Market Hall.

Before passing Watlington, the Ridgeway drops to the foot of the hills where for eight miles it remains coincident with the Upper Icknield Way, here a hedged green lane. Shirburn Hill, at 835ft/255m the highest point in Oxfordshire, is one of the imposing downland shoulders it passes. The hill is seen here from the adjacent Bald Hill – a Site of Special Scientific Interest (SSSI) – over a deep coombe where the hedge crossing its foot marks the Ridgeway. Meanwhile the ubiquitous Didcot Power Station can be made out in the far distance, centre.

Bald Hill, Shirburn Hill, the adjoining Cowleaze Wood and nearby Beacon Hill are all designated as Access Land of one sort or another, and are a favourite haunt of the red kite (*Milvus milvus*). This splendid raptor is now common in the Chilterns and is increasingly encountered on the Berkshire and Wiltshire Downs. It is distinguished not only by its forked tail and white wing patches but also by the group aerobatics in which it seems to delight. Kites were prolific in medieval times and in London were known as common scavengers. Until very recently only a relict population survived in Central Wales but with appropriate encouragement, the red kite has staged a strong and hopefully lasting comeback.

LEFT At the top of the escarpment, hidden deep in Cowleaze Wood, stands this poignant little monument. Fashioned from a redundant stone from Lincoln Cathedral, it commemorates the seven-man crew of an RAF Halifax bomber which crashed here just 6 miles from Benson, its home base, on 31 March 1944. The badly damaged plane was returning from a 1,000-bomber raid on Nuremburg. So near and yet so far.

ABOVE This is a boulder of Denner Hill Stone, the Chiltern equivalent of the sarsen stones of the Wiltshire and Berkshire Downs and formed in the same way (see pages 9–10). This particular stone sits beside Little London Wood on Beacon Hill, and may well have come to light in 1974 during the excavation of the deep M40 cutting nearby. The stone was used for general building, as cobbles and kerbs and for all sorts of utilitarian application, but most famously at Wycombe Abbey and for the late-eighteenth-century renovations of Windsor Castle. It has not been quarried at Denner Hill or elsewhere since the 1930s. The boulders were first located below ground by men with long probes before being dug out and cut up. Abandoned boulders ready for cutting can still be found scattered in the woods above Bradenham.

This picture from Beacon Hill looks to the north-east to where the Ridgeway, now lined by taller trees, marches across the fields towards Chinnor. Jutting into the vale on the right is wooded Oakley Hill, with the Chinnor chalk pits at its foot. Together with Bald Hill on the western side of the motorway, Beacon Hill is part of the Aston Rowant National Nature Reserve, and its chalk grassland is known for its rich flora, which includes numerous orchids and such rare flowers as the Chiltern gentian and wild candytuft. In the foreground are several stunted juniper bushes, another characteristic plant of the chalk downland. The old A40 highway is just out of sight as it descends the escarpment below the woods. Kingston Blount house is conspicuous in the mid-distance towards the left.

LEFT Looking north-west from the nose of Beacon Hill, the green lane, lined by low hedges and occupied by both the Iknield Way and the coincident Ridgeway, is seen crossing the middle distance. It has just passed under the Oxford-bound M40 motorway in a short tunnel. The tower of Lewknor Church is a landmark on the left.

RIGHT A horsewoman and her dog take exercise along the green lane that is both the Ridgeway and the Upper Iknield Way at the foot of the Chiltern escarpment near Kingston Blount. The wooded shoulder of Oakley Hill appears on the right. While west of the Thames the interest in horses is frequently professional, equestrianism in the Chilterns seems to be more recreational.

Between Chinnor and Princes Risborough the Ridgeway traverses Lodge Hill, which rises like a wooded island from the broad valley.

ABOVE From its foot the Ridgeway is seen coming over the fields from the shoulder of Wain Hill, where it has branched off from the Icknield Way soon after passing Chinnor. The lane passing across the picture in the middle-distance leads from Bledlow village to Bledlow Ridge up on the hill.

LEFT The steep slopes of Lodge Hill are cloaked in dense, low-growing woodland of whitebeam, hazel and beech, but the lengthy summit crest (687ft/209m) is carpeted with soft, rabbit-cropped turf. It would be a splendid place to picnic. The picture is taken looking south-west towards the northern end of the Bledlow Ridge, with Callow Hill Farm at Rout's Green in the intervening valley – a typical and almost timeless Chiltern landscape.

A casual walker exercises her dog on the Ridgeway in Giles Wood as the trail descends Whiteleaf Hill to the lonely Plough Inn at Lower Cadsden above Princes Risborough. The thickly-wooded hill, crowned by several excavated tumuli, is a popular spot although trees curtail the view. It is easily accessed from a convenient picnic site and car park.

Hampden House stands some 2 miles into the close landscape east of the Ridgeway. In its current mid-eighteenth-century Strawberry Hill Gothic incarnation, it may be familiar to some as the home of Hammer Horror Films. Earlier, however, it was the home of that great parliamentarian John Hampden 'The Patriot' (1594–1643), who as one of the Buckinghamshire MPs, defied Charles I over the Ship Money Tax in 1637, only to be arrested in this very house. During the Civil War, he was a prominent Parliamentarian leader until he was mortally wounded at the battle of Chalgrove Field. Grim's Ditch appears again in the nearby woods.

RIGHT, ABOVE Chequers, with its surrounding parkland, lies in a wide, shallow coombe between the shoulders of Coombe Hill – seen beyond the house – and the Pulpit Hill massif. It is the country retreat of the Prime Minister – whoever is in office at the time – and innumerable foreign statesmen and other notables have been entertained here as guests. Although mentioned in Domesday Book, the present house is essentially Elizabethan, having been built by its owner, William Hawtrey, in 1565. However the southern aspect – as seen in these pictures – owes much to restorations in the 1890s and in 1910, the latter for Arthur Lee, later Lord Lee of Fareham. After the First World War, Lord and Lady Lee donated the estate to the nation as a 'Thank Offering for her Deliverance in the Great War and as a place of Rest and Recreation for her Prime Ministers for ever'.

BELOW LEFT The Ridgeway trail has been carefully routed around the southern boundary of the Chequers Park, from where this picture was taken at the corner of Maple Wood. Along here the park is fenced by unusual railings cobbled together from old railway lines, doubtless very functional. Beyond, Linton's Wood clothes the escarpment leading round to Lodge Hill

BELOW RIGHT Small, somewhat explicit notices hang at frequent intervals beside the Ridgeway trail and several CCTV cameras can be spotted, especially where the Trail crosses the main drive beside the entrance lodge to Chequers.

Leaving the Chequers Valley, the Ridgeway must climb again onto the escarpment, and here at Buckmoorend the National Trail starts its steep ascent up this old wood-cutters track towards Goodmerhill Wood.

In olden times beech wood was commercially valuable, for both charcoal, firewood and furniture, and much of the beech woodland we see today has at one time been planted. Throughout the Chilterns during the eighteenth and nineteenth centuries 'bodging' – the turning and shaping of beech wood to make furniture, chair legs especially – was a cottage industry, the assembly being centred on High Wycombe, which is still a hub of the furniture business.

The Ridgeway continues through prime Chiltern beech woods for almost a mile, passing through Goodmerhill Wood and Linton's Wood, where a maze of paths are likely to complicate navigation until the occasional signpost saves the day, to Lodge Hill and the open grassy swathes of Coombe Hill beyond.

From the Ridgeway on Coombe Hill there is a last glimpse of Chequers, this time of the Elizabethan north front, standing amid its sheep-scattered parkland. Maple Wood clothes the flanks of the escarpment beyond.

The bare grassy brow of Coombe Hill (852 ft/260m), is a popular viewpoint for every man and his dog, and is easily accessible from a parking place on Lodge Hill half a mile away. The Ridgeway traverses the actual summit of Coombe Hill before setting off along the ridge to Bacombe hill and the descent to Wendover. The panorama over the Vale of Aylesbury is as magnificent as one might expect from an elevation some 500ft/150m above the fields and villages spread out below. The hill was presented to the National Trust in 1918 by Lord Lee.

BELOW LEFT The tall obelisk on the brow of the hill was built in 1904 as a monument to the Buckinghamshire men who fell in the Boer War. A plaque at the base records that it was almost totally destroyed by a lightning strike in 1938 but rebuilt by the County Council soon afterwards.

BELOW RIGHT A sailplane soars over Coombe Hill, taking advantage of the updrafts along the escarpment. Any sight of Ivinghoe Beacon, the Ridgeway's eventual destination, is blocked by the forested ridge of Aston Hill and Wendover Woods on the right of the picture.

The Ridgeway descends Wendover High Street. This charming little market town, along with Goring-on-Thames, is the only town actually astride the Ridgeway path. Granted borough status and a market in the thirteenth century, Wendover gradually expanded and in 1642 Oliver Cromwell stayed at The Red Lion, seen on the right. Today the town has a population of little more than 7,000 souls, and the market still operates, as the picture shows. At the bottom of the High Street, the Ridgeway turns sharply right in front of the 1870 Clock Tower, now a helpful information office, to ascend a narrow lane and climb once more into the hills.

The Lee is an interesting and most attractive village situated on the Chiltern tops, well back from the escarpment. Its vernacular cottages, clustered round a large village green, and its interesting provenance make it worth the short diversion from the Ridgeway. Although of ancient origin, the village was transformed a century ago by its proprietor, Arthur Lasenby Liberty, the son of a Chesham draper, who founded the celebrated Liberty's emporium in London's Regent Street. He bought the manor in 1901, demolished cottages to create the green, built the pub – The Cock and Rabbit – and several new cottages in the then contemporary Arts and Crafts style, and extended the church where he and his wife are buried. Essentially The Lee is a model village.

In rebuilding his London store in the 1920s, Arthur Liberty incorporated timbers from the last two 'wooden walls' to have been built – in 1860 – for the Royal Navy. The imposing figurehead of one, the Admiral Lord Howe, can still be seen peering over the fence at Pipers, Liberty's old mansion outside the village.

ABOVE Autumn thunder clouds gather over The Hale – a typical Chiltern view in the hill country that lies well back from the escarpment edge. The Icknield Way, following the hedge line on the right, leads to the tiny hamlet in the distance known as The Hale – just a farm and a cottage or two. Coming through the woods on the far right, the Ridgeway joins the Icknield Way a quarter of a mile beyond The Hale. On the left is the southern extremity of Wendover Woods.

LEFT An ancient sunken lane (the minor road from Cholesbury to Tring), drops down off the escarpment through Northill Woods, where a tight hairpin in the road has the intriguing name of The Crong. This view, from a path a few yards off the Ridgeway, looks over the woods above The Crong towards Ivinghoe Beacon, the end of the Ridgeway Trail, now only some 6½ miles distant as the red kite flies.

The little church of St Lawrence at Cholesbury, a village little more than a mile off the Ridgeway on top of the Chilterns, dates originally to the thirteenth century but its claim to fame is that it stands within an Iron Age hillfort, a rare situation indeed.

Despite appearing from a distance to be just a ring of tall trees, the Cholesbury hillfort is quite impressive. Enclosing a meadow area of some 10 acres is a rampart of double banks and ditches, duplicated in places and with the ditches often still 12ft/4m deep. Excavations in 1930 revealed traces of iron smelting and later Saxon occupation. The place exudes atmosphere and one can only hypothesise that perhaps our forbears built their church within the ramparts as an attempt at exorcism.

LEFT The Full Moon pub stands on the extensive village common at Cholesbury. Behind the pub stands this fine windmill. It is relatively modern, built as a smock mill in 1863 and upgraded to its current configuration as a tower mill eleven years later. It has artistic connections with the Bloomsbury Group and with J.M. Barrie and D.H. Lawrence but is now a private residence.

ABOVE The Ridgeway avoids Tring itself but passes nearby at the top of Tring Park. Purposefully sited on the old Roman Akeman Street – now the A41 – at the northern approach to the eponymous Gap, Tring is a medieval market town clustered round a steeply dipping High Street. Among its attractions is an important Zoological Museum based on the collections of Nathanial, 1st Baron Rothschild and his son Walter, the 2nd Baron, and now an outstation of the Natural History Museum in Kensington.

LEFT Purchased in 1872 by the wealthy banker Lionel Rothschild, and stocked with exotic animals by his grandson, Walter, 2nd Lord Rothschild, Tring Park – but without the animals – is now owned by the Woodland Trust.

The park encompasses the steep slopes of the Chiltern escarpment above the town and its modern A41 bypass, crossed by a convenient footbridge. The park was already extant when fully landscaped in the 1720s and its rich chalk grassland with the remnants of a fine lime avenue, sweep up to a frieze of steep woodland. Here among the tall beeches, limes, ash, yew and occasional sequoia, and just below the Ridgeway, stand two eye-catching follies, an Ionic temple and a tall obelisk – the latter dedicated to Nell Gwynn, who is said to have met Charles II in the park. Both stand at the end of long vistas between dark hedges of yew.

BELOW Beyond Tring Park the Ridgeway descends into the wide Tring Gap, which since the earliest times has been an important route northwards from the London basin. Through it, virtually side-by-side, run a main highway – originally the Roman Akeman Street – a once important canal, and the main railway line to Birmingham. In recent years, the old road has been replaced by a modern A41 highway from Watford to Aylesbury, which the Ridgeway crosses on this elegant footbridge.

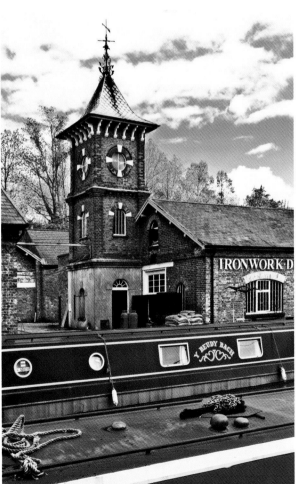

ABOVE Having crossed the A41, the Ridgeway must cross the canal and the railway, and it does both at Tring Station, which is actually some little way east of the town itself. Nearby the highest reach of the Grand Union Canal lies in a 30ft/9m deep cutting known as Tring or Cow Roast Summit – the unusual latter name taken from that of the first set of locks a short distance south.

LEFT These delightfully ornate buildings date to the mid-nineteenth century and are part of the canal-side workshops at Bulbourne, once the canal company's major repair depot and just over a mile north of the Ridgeway at Tring bridge. A small fleet of residential barges is moored here, and flights of locks let the canal and its Wendover Arm descend to lower ground.

RIGHT This stretch of the Grand Union Canal was built in the late eighteenth century as the Grand Junction Canal, reaching Tring in 1799 and completed six years later all the way to Braunston near Daventry, where several canals still converge. The cast-iron marker is a canal-side relic of the original canal company.

ABOVE The Ridgeway encounters bare chalk downland again as it traverses Pitstone Hill. This hill, rising to some 720ft/220m, is really an outlier of the continuous Chiltern escarpment which, like a higher step, rises behind, a mile to the east. Here Grim's ditch reappears briefly. Since leaving Nuffield, few vestiges of this linear earthwork have been discovered anywhere near the Ridgeway. All traces are long gone of a white horse which old records mention as having once been carved in the chalk flanks of the hill. The distant ridge in the picture is Aston Hill and Wendover Woods, above Tring.

LEFT Mentmore Towers, built in 1852 by Sir Joseph Paxton of Crystal Palace fame for Baron Meyer de Rothschild, and later the seat of Lord Rosebury, stands on an eminence 4 miles due north-west from Pitstone Hill, from where this picture was taken. A magnificent high-Victorian mansion, it is considered to be Paxton's finest surviving work. In the foreground, Pitstone Windmill stands prominently in the field in front of the village.

ABOVE Owned by the National Trust, the Pitstone Windmill is one of the oldest post mills still extant, its earliest structures dating back to 1627. It was fully restored to working order in the 1960s and the adjacent cement works, which for many years provided such an ugly and incongruous context, was demolished more recently. Standing in the fields below Pitstone Hill, the mill is a landmark for the final few miles of the Ridgeway.

RIGHT This is a winter view of Ivinghoe village from Pitstone Hill. The village lies just a mile from the foot of the eponymous Beacon on which the Ridgeway ends. It is only a small place but was once a market town held by the Bishop of Winchester and received its Royal Charter in 1318. The chalky nature of the arable land at the foot of the escarpment is very noticeable.

With Ivinghoe Beacon now
appearing attainable, just a mile
and a half ahead, the Ridgeway
enters its final lap as it descends
Pitstone Hill.

But there is one more slope to climb to the main escarpment – nearly 200 feet (60m) of ascent. However the path is not really steep and can be seen on the right above the deep coombe of Incombe Hole. Thence it continues along the scrub-scattered crest towards the Beacon itself. This last section of the Ridgeway from Tring is notably different from the previous Chiltern sections; the landform is more akin to that encountered earlier on the White Horse or Marlborough Downs.

Aldbury is a classic English village, one of the most picturesque in Hertfordshire. It stands on the shallow 'step' behind Pitstone Hill and over 250ft/75m below the crest of the main Chiltern escarpment, now steep and thickly wooded again. Aldbury boasts a village green, a pretty pond and now redundant stocks, and was once a Bridgewater estate village . In the picture The Old Manor House and Manor Cottage look out over the pond at the edge of the green.

BELOW At the top of the escarpment at an altitude of almost 600 feet (180m) stretches the National Trust's extensive Ashridge estate. The notable landmark here, towering over the woods which tumble over the escarpment edge, is the Bridgewater Monument, erected in 1832 to commemorate the great canal pioneer – Francis the 3rd Duke of Bridgewater. Designed by Sir Jeffrey Wyatville and a full 108 feet (33m) in height, the viewing platform at the top is reached by 170 steps. The inscription at the base of the tall Doric column dubs the Duke, quite correctly, as 'The Father of Inland Navigation'.

LEFT Inside Aldbury's thirteenth-century church of St John the Baptist are some superb medieval brasses and also these magnificent effigies of Sir Robert Whittingham and his wife, dated 1471. Sir Robert wears full armour and his feet rest on a strange Wild Man armed with a club. The shadowed marble busts on the wall behind commemorate Sir Richard and Lady Anderson, the seventeenth-century owners of Sir Robert's Pendley estate near by.

Ivinghoe Beacon; this picture shows the last, steep, 500 yards to the summit, a hardly-demanding 80ft/24m of ascent. The 790ft/240m hill feels out on a limb, aloof and open to the winds – as indeed it is. Blowing grass, scrubby juniper bushes and patches of bare chalk characterise its slopes and render it a fitting conclusion to the Ridgeway. The Beacon attracts many visitors but nevertheless it seems a pity that a metalled lane with designated parking spots crosses its shoulder, for Ivinghoe Beacon deserves to be more remote.

Except in two places, steep slopes encircle the Beacon. One is the broad south ridge by which the Ridgeway – and indeed most people – ascend, the other is the beckoning grassy crest which extends for a half mile due east. The shape and ambiance of this spur is such that any aesthetically-minded hill-lover will be tempted to traverse it to Gallows Hill, as the far end is known. In this picture the east ridge is seen pointing over the intervening valley to the well-known Dunstable Lion chalk figure. Carved into the slope of the Dunstable Downs across the county divide in Bedfordshire, the white lion marks virtually the final manifestation of the Chiltern Hills.

Select Bibliography

Chilterns & Ridgeway Rambler's Guide by Martin Andrew
(HarperCollins, 2001)
Exploring the Ridgeway by Alan Charles (Countryside Books, 1992)
The Ridgeway National Trail Guide by Neil Curtis (Aurum Press, 1994)
Discovering the English Lowlands by Martin Andrew & John Cleare
(Crowood Press, 1991)
The Mountain Biker's Guide to the Ridgeway by A. Bull & F. Barrett
(Stanley Paul, 1991)
The Oldest Road by J.R.L. Anderson & Fay Godwin (Whittet Book,
1987)
The Ridgeway Path by Hugh Westacott & Mark Richards (Penguin,
1982)

The very useful National Trail website can be found at:
http://www.nationaltrail.co.uk/Ridgeway

Maps

OS Explorer 1:25,000 scale
    Sheet 157 Marlborough
    Sheet 170 Abingdon, Wantage & Vale of White Horse
    Sheet 171 Chiltern Hills West
    Sheet 181 Chiltern Hills North

OS Landranger 1:50,000 scale
    Sheet 165 Aylesbury & Leighton Buzzard
    Sheet 173 Swindon & Devizes
    Sheet 174 Newbury & Wantage
    Sheet 175 Reading & Windsor

Harvey Maps : 1:40,000 scale
    The Ridgeway: a dedicated, single sheet, waterproof map

Index